With Nothing behind but Sky

PERIE LONGO

POEMS

With Nothing behind but Sky

a journey through grief

ARTAMO PRESS

SANTA BARBARA · CALIFORNIA

Published by
ARTAMO PRESS

First edition, 2006
Copyright © 2006 by Perie Longo

Permissions acknowledgements appear on page 6.

Artamo Press is a division of Artamo LLC.

Book and cover design by Jack N. Mohr

Library of Congress Control Number: 2006933900
ISBN-13: 978-0-9788475-0-0
ISBN-10: 0-9788475-0-4

www.artamopress.com

Printed on acid-free paper in the United States of America

In memory of Phil

ACKNOWLEDGMENTS

The author gratefully acknowledges the following publications where several of these poems first appeared:

Into The Teeth of The Wind (vol. 4, #1): "The Widow Thinks about Eyeglasses"; *Journal of Poetry Therapy* (Vol. 15, #4): "Checking In"; *King Log 7*: "The Widow Rubs up against Her Limits" and "The Widow Confronts Skunks in the Middle of the Night"; *Phantasmagoria* (2006): "A Crossing"; *Rattle* (#12, #17, #19): "The DAR's Daughter," "While Watching a Video of the Dalia Lama," "The Widow Discovers Her Tires Are Bald When the 'Check Engine' Light Comes On"; *Rivertalk* (1999, 2002, 2003, 2003): "Squoze," "Not Counting," "Chinese Elm," "The Widow Attempts a Singles' Group Potluck"; *Solo 7* (2004): "This Then Today"; *Solo Café 2* (2006): "Goldilocks"; *The Cancer Poetry Project: Poems by Cancer Patients and Those Who Love Them* (FAIRVIEW PRESS, 2001): "Chores"; *The Healing Fountain: Poetry Therapy for Life's Journey* (NORTH STAR PRESS, 2003): "Sometimes a Life."

The author also wishes to acknowledge the editing assistance and support of David Starkey and Lisa Meckel, and all those in her Sunday poetry group, as well as her family and friends for their unending patience and sustenance during her journey that led to these poems. Special gratitude is given to Jack N. Mohr and Elvira Monika Laskowski-Caujolle of Artamo Press for publishing this work.

CONTENTS

PART I

A Crossing

Never clean the garage if your motorcycle
needs to get its weekly exercise.

Saturday is a day to test yourself against the wind
up your back, down your neck,
between your legs, the colder the better.

Never sit still if there's a mountain to climb —
by foot or on horseback —
especially if you're after the highest peak in the U.S.,
no matter if your boots fit or not.

Definitely never spend the day removing dust   8/96
if there are good swells for sailing, the higher the better.
You know how big you are if you ride them out
and when the boat starts sinking,
call the coast guard who always comes, if you believe.

Risking your life is a good thing — it halts rumination.
Women ruminate too much and want compliments
and affection for no reason, but push
come to shove, when our child was ill,

my husband walked me through my rage and fear,
never walked out, never said stop it.
He said she would be all right, can I get you anything?
And took me hiking. When water ran out
a creek appeared and we nestled down until the sun
left the face of the rock and I wept.

Stay together if possible.
Travel to islands practically off the map and be renewed.
Even do yoga at the edge of piers and sing
as much as you can.

Cat Scan

In a dream I rescued the cat
on the way out of a war torn town,
where we really do not live. I noticed my cat
was not my cat, only pretended to be.
When I awake next morning I say to you
you are not really a man with a white cell count
reaching dangerous limits, lymphocytes
running through your veins
like people running from the din of guns.
You are a healthy man who loves red wine.
You just put on the wrong face like our cat
in my dream and we will live happily ever after,
really. But today the doctor points out
on your cat scan the bulge of white lymph nodes
like miniature mushrooms, H-bombs exploding
against a dark background that leaves us stunned.

11/96

I don't think you should take
another person's word for it,
but I learned if you hang in there
a long time you come out the other side,
and it's not just the other side
as the bear saw, but meadows of wildflowers
with a log cabin on the edge, logs for winter stacked
along the south side. You have to earn your fires,
burn bridges — so here we are, surprise surprise —
an unholy team, walking on water,
eyes gazing between the slats
and still
above it all where a liquid tongue
lunges over the mountain, cracks
over jagged granite meant to snap you awake.
Even with sore muscles we managed
to climb to another height
and yes, take my word for it,
with something we learned
along the way, love.

10/97

I wish I could name everything;
the bushes of upside down golden flowers
with red centers lining a friend's driveway,
shrimp colored bells rising from sage green bowls.
Brittle leaves hugging the rocks.
The feeling beside a creek when I tumble down
or the sound of a fly that penetrates the silence
of a July morning. If I could name the fear
I sometimes have you will be gone one day,
what would I call it — alone
like the wind as it rushes past everything,
or still as the stick which once bloomed?

7/98

Squoze

Down Highway 15 past Vegas
past midnight inside the steam
of air you say you are "squoze."
I wonder what that means.
You take your hands off the wheel
and press them together as in prayer,
repeat the word "squoze"
while the RV slides a little to the left.
"Squozen," I correct, grabbing
the wheel, unsure of this form
as yours, squoze as we are between two trucks,
just a pebble sucked between forces
of steel and rubber.

Holding my breath, heat rising
from the road through the floorboards
burning my bare feet, a water bottle
held between my legs,
fatigue trying to squeeze me
from one state to the next,

I think squozen a good word,
what happens to your life at the end
when you're trying to squeeze in
as much as you can, pushing to the rim.

So here we are beside each other
headed home from putting your father
to rest in the earth of his home,

7/98

squoze from comfort and our bed
in a rickety RV plugging away like we have
for more than a few years, semi's blasting us
on either side. You let them have their way
and as I have trusted you always, whatever
is said, I lean back for a snooze, your word
stretching its arms into the long night.

THE CHANGING SEASON

The weatherman said fall occurred at 12:12 p.m.
yesterday, but the calendar said it was Monday.
Maybe only the sun and moon know
in their serious liaison gone on for millenniums

and here I am boasting about our marriage
continuing thirty years. I don't know
how that happened or how light and dark
can be exactly equal twice a year,
as we were never equally divided on anything

but we have fallen into some rhythm
to baffle the gods, bowing to each other
in our ups and downs, clearing out
when the reptilian brain takes charge, laughing
at each other's irritations when once they were cause for war.

I only know fall is here because your smile
reminded me of marigolds when you came home
yesterday, opened a seasonless meadow in me
which could lead us right into winter
whatever the odds.

9/98

Rain coming, clouds elephant-hide gray,
your Harley chugging
like its been through a few battles,
we arrive at the vineyard.
You switch off the engine.
I hop off, my backside aching
from every buckle in the road.
Streets of green vines beckon.
Seconds flat, I am in their arms,
notice clumps of hidden fruit,
reach in and nestle the plump grapes,
small eggs, caviar of time.

10/98

Like a young child I call to you to come see,
as if the discovery isn't true unless shared.
You meander down the aisle toward me
in your leathers, behind you the Harley leaning
against the tired sky.

I take your hand and place it under the tender fruit,
a good thing for us, dusty odd couple
on their anniversary, holding on.

His illness had taken over our lives
like one of those alligators in the living room
I read about in books exploring why your life
is so fucked-up. I'm not sure I can use the word
"fuck" in a poem and still be allowed
to be a member of the Poetry Society of America,
even though it sounds accurate. Moreover, my mother
who was a Daughter of the American Revolution,
might come back and disown me, she who made it clear
in my upbringing we were special
and never used such common language.

6/99   One day when I had matured enough to ask
what this relative did in the revolution, instead
of storming out with "oh not that again,"
she said with her head held high, though a little sheepish,
that he carried a lantern. I could appreciate that,
a great-great-great something-or-other who lit the way
so soldiers wouldn't stumble all over themselves
but fall neatly to the side should they pass out
or even die.

So that's what I came to do, cancer or not,
told the family this was the only life we had and together
we better find a way to fight even beyond seeing
the whites of their eyes, or for that matter
those common white cells.
And when it became the darkest, I lit
the kerosene lamp on the mantle

with a sense of purpose and paraded through the house shouting, "All is well, all is well."

Tomorrow I will honor the curve
of a leaf, any leaf and how the sun
falls on a mass of daisies laid down
in plenty on my garden floor. Tomorrow
I will tie them up and call my sister,
I promise myself, tell her it is all right she
doesn't know what to say about my beloved
being so ill — we can't be wise always,
but we can allow silence to draw us
together. From his hospital bed, my husband
tells me about a little girl he saw skipping down
the hall so full of life, to watch for her,
7/99   and then she appears again bopping along,
her braids bouncing, socks slipping.
She peeks, just a sliver of a glance,
through the door, clicks her fingers, then
hums off. Isn't that it? Helping each other notice
each day why the sun really rises?

Tomorrow will he be stronger?
Tonight will his fever rise again like the tide
beaching him in the ocean of himself?
Tomorrow will I have the energy to wash away
what his body casts off, the energy to hope
when his eyes wander outside to meet
the generosity of tree and sky?

My friend writes I should look
at the moon and stars each night. She means
to offer me strength, but how do
mere humans continue?

8/99

Tonight the cicada is too loud.
How can it hold one note that long
without taking a breath?

How can I hold our lives alone like this,
he over in his chair gathering himself
while I stir the pot, get this and that,
one eye looking into the dark,
the other on the stove. I step outside
to cut a rose for him.

The cicada begins to sing again.

To Be True in a Moment

It is difficult to be true in a moment
you have never been true in before.
A clever script would be helpful,
a dress rehearsal. We could wear
charming period pieces to take away
the bite, he in a blue waist coat
with one of those canoe looking hats,
me in a hoop skirt and décolletage top.
He would be headed into battle, while I
would cling to his white stockinged ankles
begging *don't leave me like this.*

8/99   This is untrue.

He would be in his worn T-shirt from Mexico,
a baseball cap emblazoned with *Harley Rules*
and I in my thin terry robe, like tonight,
a full moon above the reflection of a sunflower
in the window, their roundness similar,
as if to remind me life and death are two sides
of the same coin. Heads or tails no one flips.

Thank you for not dying,
for giving me your strong arm
as we walk down the cheerful street,
not quite as chipper as the young couple
clothed in black, kissing, their faces all light.
So what if we are the oldest pedestrians.
Our steps are not taken lightly
nor our breath, every act filled with
indescribable meaning I can feel
when my lip quivers at the corner
while we wait for the light to change.
You look straight ahead. I look at you.
Everything stops.   11/99

For seven days we squeezed past our Noble's fir body
wearing nothing but lights and one angel on top, but
finally my daughter and I hung ornaments. I loved especially
the wooden ones my stepson made when he was 10.
Bored with pneumonia, he painted each one
with loving precision; the dove, the camel, the soldier
and train. Through all the unwrapping of gifts, he smiled
though he never got what he wanted most, his mother alive,
and here he is again, his father not feeling too well.

As I removed each ornament I decided this next century
I would be organized, like nature — all the trees
leaning into the wind, all the water going down stream.
Each rock right where it was intended.
The sun up above the round mountains.
Two hawks circling above the pines.
When we put up another tree, I want everything labeled,
everything in its place, every memory hanging
where we can reach it.

12/99

My husband has fallen in love with his doctor,
the one with long golden curls
who orders up this or that chemical, this or that
blood component to raise one part, lower another.
He calls her Goldilocks.
I bring newspapers and milkshakes.
He calls me nothing,
my coming and going an irritation

while he is tethered to infusion bags,
fastened to a tall stand he pushes along
while we amble down the hall for exercise.
Such insult for two hikers who have reached   5/00
several mountain peaks weighted down with packs.
Here the going is harder.

"Have you acted like a bear yet?"
I ask, peeling paper from the straw,
inserting it through the slit in the lid of the shake.
He growls.
Liquid amber runs — just right —
into his veins. I am not jealous of Goldilocks.
She can save him. Little wonder women
turn the other way
when their partners don't return at night.
Life sometimes has these prices.

Late May, husband ill again, I miss
planning for a summer trip, loading
the car with tent and cooler, ground cloths,
camp stove, repellent, back packs —
fussing to adjust the fit — necessities compressed
for comfort once you hit the road. How I love
the meditation of asphalt and fir trees,
yellow lines that lengthen with each
horizon met, remember how sky
enters yawn, ears, how it sneaks under
arm pits in the heat, down the contours
of breast, belly, how I think you've gone too far,
6/00   sky, getting into everywhere.
Fire shoots from my mouth.
I am in the river swimming
and it all starts again with the water,
insects in hair, dragonflies so close
I can see through the gauze of their wings
to the opposite bank where my children,
my skies my suns my moons, wait
for me. *Go* I tell them, before it is too late,
get down that road and let me know
the color of mud under your fingernails
early in the morning when you get the fire going
with numb fingers, while you wait
for the kettle to boil, a scuffle of wild tracks
around your site before you start your climb.

How are you
         not too well — fever again

The doctor said you'd live
         the treatment will kill the fungus
         if it doesn't kill me first

Don't say that
         how are you

Okay — mailed your disability claim
ears stuffed up (maybe with what
I don't want to hear)   6/00
         sorry to hear that

It's nothing I'll be fine
the sun is out
(driving home I saw
purple jacaranda against
sailor blue sky cloud mountains
so beautiful) I wish I wish
         talk to you later

I love you
         me too

do you need anything
         nothing else

Remission

I've been writing too much about his illness,
    the beast that came into his blood one year
when he looked out his window at work,
    in the shadow of a nuclear plant built for future needs,
he thinking it would be a good day to go fishing,
    the sky blue, air filled with toxins
he could not know about. I don't want to think about that,
    want to notice how the brilliant orange of the
    honeysuckle
        opens itself to the sun,
        as the son opens to the father,
enters our front door calling my name,

6/00

        me the one who has no answers
but understands the woe of seeing a father wilted
    on a bed of white.

    I want to hear that bird again,
    that delirium — about the sky is it?
    or a worm? Or the coolness of clustered banana leaves?

I remind my son just yesterday the doctor said
his father's lymph nodes had shrunk from the size of apricots
to raisins. My son looks at me in his steady way
    that holds you, like a flashlight in the dark.

When I heard the news I wanted to throw off my clothes
and run down State Street, I tell him,
> but I was on the cell phone turning left, a policeman
> on the corner, me without a seat belt, so I just smiled
> and waved and kept going.
>   Green reaches in.

Sometimes it's hard to stick to the subject.
Sometimes that's all you do.

The Waiting Room

To pass the time, waiting
for the surgeon to report
how my husband fared under
his skilled hand, I read
the newspaper about the genome,
how in the future doctors will turn a little screw,
so to speak, of a certain gene,
twist a glitch to stall
the inevitable, improve on God a bit.

Next page there is a photo
of the wonder-drug septuplets
6/00   now 2 ½ years old, all slipped
from the same pod, parents smiling
sure the two most frail will walk.
I am grateful, but wonder
as science draws us further into perfection,
won't something be missing —

A lot of spleen, the surgeon reports,
words chiseled, *jostled a few organs*
to get it out.

Everything seems removed.

When I see him later, this is not the man
I know, have been young and daring with,
have hung off cliffs with,
had children with, been holy and unholy with
and yet it is and I am outside.

All I can do is moisten his lips with a small sponge
dipped in ice water, not too much —
tell him how well he did, thirsty as he is.

A Crossing

Sometimes we talk about the time
we almost lost our lives at sea —
you, me, our son, and friends —

how great swells came from nowhere
as if Poseidon himself had risen for air,
water overpowering us as we slid in the troughs

our fear so immense I wished for Jonah's whale
to gather us up in one large gulp,
no matter how dark or sharp

7/00   the edges, just to stop the pitch of boat
against the splinters of ourselves.
Somehow you steered us out, Captain,

saved our lives and now here we are
twenty years past. What lies ahead
seems more formidable

despite the brilliant sky. I am lost
to save you back, but if I could walk you
straight out of this hospital, I would —

even dressed in that miserable polka-dot gown.
We'd wheel the Sisyphus IV mount
onto the elevator and ride the wave of it down

to ground floor, march into the fierce wind,
and with a Poseidon size laugh pull out each tube,
not so much for where we were going

but for where we'd been, telling all
the good times over and over, even today,
how the good nurses ran after us. How traffic stopped

so we could cross.

I remember the summer we first rafted
down the river, whatever its name, just out of Moab.
I was bored, hearing the leader drone on about the history
of the shore trees, whatever their name,
how they were draining the river
and would have to be removed.
I was bored with the cliffs, red and all alike,
so when the guide asked if anyone wanted to paddle the kayak
through the rapids I said *yes, me, yes.*
I took the lead, you not knowing what to make of it,
how to sit there, behind, for balance
and let me go, let me guide us smack into the rapids.
I remember leaning into your spread legs,
tight into you, so when the churning came,
when there was only slipping into troughs and out,
in and out, I realized to forge ahead
you become the water, ride it, let it toss you,
let it bring you down,
let it float you
so here we are floating, my love,
just before the rapids again
riding your illness. It's hard to say
what's happening while we paddle like hell.

12/00

Today at lunch my grown son
folds a candy wrapper into a small boat —
point to point, crease, unfold, refold —
like we used to make from newspapers
on rainy days when he was five.
I loved creasing the news of world disasters
into those Curious George boats
my son would fill with his miniature animals
and float in the rain
as it streamed along the curbs.
I'd be holding an umbrella over him
but when you're five in command
of a fleet of boats as they rush
down a river carrying treasures
you don't want your mother there
protecting you from the very thing
you were born for. And so I became the crew.
We'd rescue his boats at the sewer
where the river rain spilled to the sea,
run up the street and begin all over again.

He hands me the boat
across the table on Valentine's Day.
The mountains are covered with snow,
one of those days when rescue is everything
and time folds over itself,
when a heart knows what it is to be full,
and you feel you could float forever.

2/01

Palm Sunday

Death has come to bed with me,
wakes me up, blinds me to spring flowers
spilling over the back fence.

Look what you have done
to my husband's body, our minds, I say,
how you have hung life out of reach
from the tree outside our window.

There is one thing.
How I shaved him yesterday
for the first time
and noticed how tough his beard,
how afraid I was to push too hard,
how his eyes glazed.

At least they are open
I tell myself,
and point out how smooth the sky.

4/01

my azaleas rise from the dead
making a liar of me,
my somberness about death

    how thick it is,
    mud-after-flood thick.

The azaleas are shades of dawn sky,
bare-yourself-to-me pink.

    I bathe him with honey soap,
    stroke his face, across his shoulders, back,
    chest, under his arms, down his chest,
    between his legs, down his legs.
    He looks the other way.

4/01

They rub against each other,
as if to say how beautiful they are
to each other.

    Ours is the language of fog.
    We plod through mud, fall
    to our knees the second, tenth,
    thirteenth time.

    I adjust his pillows, bring water laced
    with the *elixir of life*, the blue bottle reads,
    broth diluted, not too salty.
    As I read aloud from a new western novel
    he rises and gallops off with the posse
    after the enemy, never minding
    the sun in his eyes.

HOME AGAIN TONIGHT

Always I have tried to meet
your challenges, but tonight
with infusion lines in your arms
two capped nodules dangling
where the good blood goes
the chemo the antibiotics
I understand what I can
when you say *I have no comfort*
stroke your hand bruised
where blood has lost its way
place my hand on your heart
beating under the old blue and white
5/01   checkered pajamas and pat it
speechless
even though I want to remind you
of our children the sea the mountains
the octopus in Fiji you studied
under the end of the pier each dawn
loving the gentle way its arms coiled
and uncoiled as it fed
the curves of all those roads
we traveled on your Harley
how cold we were and comfort came —

when I place my ear on your heart, hoping,
I hear the sound of hissing snakes,
how it races a little faster with mine —
life still with us tonight
which we can make last a very long time.

A quiet swing up the 210 cuts through the canyon,
frees me to get from one side of L.A. to the other
and home a little more quickly. I wonder how she is
contained back there
in that brown carton.
It's a hell of a note, my husband near death,
me, wife number two, all fire and brimstone
driving his first wife's ashes to our house
after thirty-two years,
the one I should be more like, subdued.

One morning, boys going off to school, she just stopped
breathing. A ruptured stomach   5/01
the autopsy said.
A doe she was, heart of gold,
I'm told, couldn't take how life
twisted itself around corners.

I hardly breath, carrying out his wish
to have her dug up from the old gravesite,
cremated, moved to the family plot 1500 miles away.
What's it like to be lifted from the dark
into all this light and rush?
Does the spirit spit or swear?
Does it matter the body's dust be returned
to its home town? But my husband
wants this as he wants himself
set in the earth of his childhood,
before bad luck brought us here,

before he knew I would do whatever it took
for him to rest in peace.

44

When I carry her into the house
I don't say *here she is*
or ask where to put her. I don't
say anything. He doesn't either, holding on.
I'm holding her as if she were a trophy, the one
I should have been more like.
The garage is too cold. I could put them together
and sleep in the guest room.
But I don't.

The Slant of Green Shadows

Back from death's door, my love skims
the latest *New Yorker*. On the cover a woman
dances toward the sea, her tossed-off dress
a kite in the breeze. I wonder if he dreams
                    to catch her.

        I am reading a novel about Vermeer,
how he taught his maid clouds
were not really white, that she should look hard
                    to see the true colors.

        A monitor tracks his heartbeat
more green than any spring hill after winter rain.
An oblong window, behind his bed, reveals sky
not blue but what is left
                    when our seeing runs out.

        His feet are blue, I told them
but they said it was nothing,
lack of exercise lying in bed so much.
                Purple as storm clouds,
I argued, with thunder and rain in them.
They rushed him to surgery, afraid
                    he might lose a leg.

        He tells me I am beautiful
when I move his swollen legs elevated
on pillows almost white like the snow
we hiked through only three summers ago high
in the Tetons. I want to remember

5/01

the light at our feet when we sat on a rock
and let darkness out of an orange,
sticky and clear as it trickled down our chins.
How we looked down the mountain
at all the waterfalls, the slant of green shadows
                        from which we'd risen.

What Good

Though your eyes had been closed
most of two days

        (what made me think
        you would wake up and go about your life)

on the early morning of the third day
just before your breath slowed
as if sucking air through scuba gear

more slowly then
pauses   too long   between each sip

your eyes opened wide, unblinking,
lifted upward, not as far as the ceiling,
just above my head.

Did you see the light
or the tunnel? Your parents?
I wondered if you saw God.

If so, what good was it to ask the nurses
each time they came in
the night before, our last together,
as I slept on a cot at the foot of your bed,

what good was it as they rolled you
from one side to the other
off your sore red spine

        (as the beached seal rolls —
        as the sea)
to ask if you were all right?

6/24/01

Of course you were, if you saw God.
You have need for nothing else
as I do.

PART II

AFTER A GREAT LOSS

Sometimes the world is too large to fit on a page,
the woods eventually closing us out. I must stop
giving myself these impossible tasks.

Sometimes a life is too much to fit on a page.
I tried today, tried to describe his coming
and going, our laughing and weeping.

Sometimes a day is too complicated to fit on a page,
how it suddenly changes from bursts of red trees
to gray. Best to not talk about love.

Sometimes a love is too grand to fit on a page.   UNDATED
It needs a country to contain its edges and alleys,
not an open woods filled with bears and high peaks.

Let us be dark for a while. Sometimes you need
a whole night to weep. After all, the moon is full
and the world once too large to fit on this page
                has become terribly small.

A Better Place

— to a neighbor

Do they make love better in heaven
or is everyone above it all?

If God's presence makes heaven preferable,
what do you call it
when your beloved looks inside
        and you feel expanded beyond pain?

I'd let him go if he could have strong legs
        and a steep slope with snow that flies
into his face as he races down, looking over
his shoulder to make sure
I'm there.
I'd let him go for the perfect road
where he could bend with his Harley
painted with gaudy flames.

And if I could send him his piano
and harmonicas and Charley Musselwhite blues harp
song book and red concertina,

if I could send him his favorite Hawaiian shirts
and his side of the bed
with both of us waking together on a Sunday morning
and two scrambled eggs laced with cheese
and pancakes with pure maple syrup and KCBX
playing some blue grass
        and he'd write a note back,
I'd let him go, I would.

7/01

ONE MONTH LATER

It's all the same thing,
God birth death life old clothes
stuffed in grocery bags,
shirts that comforted his skin,
skin that comforted mine,
thin jeans he wore
when he changed the oil in his Harley,
those souvenir baseball caps
stacked on the hat tree
collected from all the far away places.
I get up eat dress walk eat read
write thank you notes
garden sweep sort run weep.   7/01
He can't even see how well
I'm not managing.
I light a candle beside his picture
and watch the flame sway.
Maybe he'll see it and wave back.

Circling around Golden Gate Park
— for my daughter

You bring me to a place that gives you
          peace
though we walked in circles to find it,
past roses and tea gardens and gnarled trees
twisted around themselves that arch over us
as we make our way out
          of the storm,

your father's illness a claw
that pressed in for months, the swells
of his doing well/not doing well
taking us off course so we barely knew
ourselves. Then one Sunday morning

he left us with barely a sigh,
left us dangling on slippery ground.
But here we are at the shore of the lake, steady,
ducks skimming by, some asleep
in the shade of branches.

      Centered here
we speak about how to go on
like the traffic that starts and stops,
check the map to see where we are
as we watch two hawks circling,
        circling and remember
how well your father
taught us how to travel.

7/01

Two Months Later

Each time I pass the picture of him
leaning against a pine tree
high in the mountains
a white straw hat covering his head
I notice the light from his eyes
and touch him, touch
the spirit of him that twirls
when he has a mind to come inside
like now, I can tell, how the cat meows
into the middle of the room,
how I lean against air.

8/01

Everything I see or hear is about him
since he has been gone.
This morning, the Dalai Lama
says there is so much suffering
in the world he can't do much.

With his monks he sifts colored sand
into an intricate design for peace,
then sweeps it away. They collect
the remains in a small jar, sprinkle a little
on top of their heads for tranquility.

8/01 While I held my husband in my hands
as ash, like finest sand,
all the hard edges of us disappeared
with the smoke. I rubbed him on my skin

then flew him into light.

Such tragedy! how it takes death
to put everything in its right place,
how it takes death to perfect a life.

Strange I had not been counting
the numbers of days or hours
so when a friend asked how long
since he passed away
a huge silence fell over me unlike
the middle of night when even coyotes
have ceased their yipping, their ripping
at some feeble prey about its business
sniffing and wiggling its tail.

How many candles lit,
how many times the door locked and then
unlocked, how often had I noticed
hummingbirds come to sip
the honeysuckle in our garden
since his last breath went out to join
the coyote's and foghorn's moan,
the fog itself.

I think I told her I lost count.
Some of us don't, you know,
don't keep track. It keeps him closer,
along with the lit candle,
the unlocked door, just in case.

11/01

Sweeping Leaves in a Serious Wind

Capturing the first layer
of leaves like the first draft
of a poem on fire before it blows away,
I think of Octavio Paz who said
our poems drift in the air.

I sweep them into a bag,
some painted with summer heat,
some with the sunken sun, others blemished
with a disease I have forgotten
as I forget sickness of any kind.
All are veined where life had its way.

11/01

Those from the African Fern Pine
are needles, memories that cling —
how he held on minute after minute.
I sweep them into the bag, all our days collected,
not just the last. How surprising

the full bag is light,
how he looks over my shoulder as I struggle,
tells me to wrap a corner
around the back of a lawn chair
and fasten it with a clothespin
as he used to.

The more leaves I sweep,
the more come down.
There is not enough room.
A wind runs up my spine and doesn't stop.

SIX MONTHS LATER

light
lights
light

— Raymond Rosliep (1917–83)

I questioned celebration this December,
whether it was fitting, when I noticed
how the last red rose in my garden
leaned into the light of winter chill.

12/01

We decided: at least a tree,
found one, small and lopsided. After all,
my daughter said, who ever saw
a perfect one in the wild.

We faced its wide space toward the room
where anyone could see the problem.
There we hung his favorite ornament, a sailboat
which sways when the heat comes on,

when our vision begins to dim.
He's there, we think, slipping between
the branches, the angels, this life
and the next blended in woven lights.

Visitation

Christmas morning, a ping at the window
and another, ping ping —
I think a pebble

cast from the hand of a child to draw me
from sleep, rejoice

at something important learned
from dream. Awake, I see
it is a golden bird, small and insistent

wanting seed? warmth? his side
of the bed? my eternally absent mate
returned to quicken my heart?

I jump to the window
but it flits away like all elusive things.

Last morning of the year it comes again
after the rain. Ping ping — I am prepared
having snipped a lone narcissus
from the yard

stood it in a vase
straightened the stand where I keep his picture,
a candle, a crystal to catch stray light.

These enticements are not enough
to keep him here, this ghost

cloaked in the color of sun
I walk into, awake and willing
to transform at any time.

12/01

Opened the brambled honeysuckle mouth
to the sea's stormy breath,
hacked down branches of the pitosporum
for the sky's variance,
sawed off the bottom limbs of the pines
so you can find my house if you want to.

Death has taken up too much time.
Even he said it from his perch on the mantle.

Now this. I bagged his shoes, I did,
and his ties like sorry thin prayer flags
dangling from the bedroom door.   1/02
I saved the one with the mallard ducks
he liked to wear with his tweed jacket,
the natty look I called it, for a man of the bench
who really wanted to be out in a canoe
watching ripples of small things on the move.

How could I tell my family no valentine
for me, back in fourth grade?

What made me chase after a red paper heart
with ruffled white edge, in the bitter wind?

In the center of the heart, an inscription in pencil —
"To: _______", easy to erase
and print darkly my name.

Somehow this memory led as I walked
through dusk today, the first February 14th
without my love of years, no card or flowers
or splurge of desire, feeling invisible as then
back in the bitter wind. Then truly,
from the top of an oak broke
a red balloon lifting against
the whiteness of sky, its string a cord

to my heart, this red message
writing his name across the air
I could not chase, only stare as it grew
out of sight while crows raised their cry.

2/02

THE WIDOW DISCOVERS HER TIRES ARE BALD
WHEN THE "CHECK ENGINE" LIGHT COMES ON

Just days before he slipped off, he asked
if I had the loose piece of side chrome attached,
the oil changed, he didn't want his car falling apart,
never mind me, the unmechanical one, who rode this life
alongside him, each with our own separate tasks
and now they're all mine. I think the car might need oil
again, like I could use, some zip, but can't figure out
where the hood latch is. On my knees, I squeeze my head
under the driving wheel panel, such a mystery of gadgets,
so many mysteries to solve to keep things running in his loss.
No latch to be found I sit back on my heels,
then notice the tires are almost bald,   3/02
something like my hair coming out in clumps these months,
and wonder how that happened overnight. I barely
go anywhere while he just up and vanishes —
with no directions. Maybe he's been traveling
while I sleep, letting the good times roll.

What Good These Lists

On sticky yellow post-its
plastered to the cupboards, phone,
dashboard, reminders of what's needed:
cat food, ginger tea,
Tues. PM. 7:30 Ch.19 —
though I don't say what I am to watch.

Remembering the notes is a trick.
The other day I bought a dust cloth
instead of light bulbs,
struck numb in the household section
grabbing at anything useful.
And I needed to dust
having arrived at the conclusion
it is sacred,
       something like the cow in India,

most likely the remains
of all our loved ones come home
to lie on the mantle
the piano
the table
      in peace.

I run my finger lightly
over the film
leaving a road for him
to find me,
the one I cared for as if
he were my own.

4/02

A WHOLE OTHER THING

When they die, it's a whole other thing.
— Gail Rink, Hospice executive director

Up until now I thought if I kept light
around his face, the invitation of flowers
at his feet, he would return.

Month after month goes by and still
no word. My enticements grow
further apart, but yesterday I could not resist

pushing open the back gate
to get to the other side of the fence
where wisteria spilled its mauve heart

toward the wide field. Gathering several sprays
into my arms, I knew he was somewhere
if I could only see.

In a dream he plays the piano
as in life, *them bones them dry bones,*
hear the word of the Lord and I who can't sing

sang in my swamp voice, surprisingly in tune.
We looked at each other just once, satisfied.
The house is sweet again.

4/02

RUINS: PISAC, PERU

1

Come from a year of grief into a mysterious land
high in the Andes, yearning for adventure,
some escape from sympathy and a mountain of boxes.
My head throbs in the thin air,
        or the struggle in my dream,

how my husband appeared from the other side
to help me bring our boat to dock under fierce winds.
Even then I rammed it into a wall of rocks,
my skill no match for the force. He didn't complain
of the wound in his leg when we crashed,

looked through me, and though I placed my hand
where he bled, it grew larger,
bleeds red into the morning here in Pisac.
A mountainside slants through the window,
its frame painted red.

I am not at sea after all,
notice how calla lilies open to the sun,
lick warmth with yellow tongues. Beyond, patches
of stubbled wheat and corn square against each other
        in winter's chill. Everywhere, wild mint.

5/02

2

We drive through the Sacred Valley
along the River Urubamba raging with earlier storms
to the ruins at Ollantaytambo. Our Indian guide
turns his tongue around the history of the Inca walls,
a mystery how each massive stone was cut in several angles,
to fit like a puzzle
            into the next,
to hold strong without mortar over 7,000 years.

This is the wall of my dream.
I run my hand along the impossible.
Press fingers into crevices. Here the dead
can live in shadows.

            I could not stop the storm of his decline,
            only refuse autopsy, his sacrifice enough.

We follow the voice of our guide up to the altar
of the sacrificed. He whispers
with reverence. Once the centers of virgins were removed,
they were trussed with wild mint
before wrapped in sacred cloths, wound around, around
not for display in museums, no.
To be wed to earth.

He picks mint from the ground at our feet,
rubs it between his fingers, lifts it for us to breathe.

> I remember the disinfectant that did no good,
> the sterile white walls. Better mint
> than infused red blood, near the end.
> Better a mountain top.

And then as if in a dream, from the heights of the ruins
a man steps out playing a familiar song on his flute —
el condor pasa — and it does, this bird
of the Inca's upper world, sails down, wraps around
and around us all, time has us in its shadow, preserves us.
Then it passes,
> and we are free to move on.

SNAKESKIN

> — for Paul (January 23, 1961 – June 6, 2002)

Wondering where he could have gone,
this step-son, this brother,
my daughter and I walk up the hill
between the woods
and the rest of the world

barely real under the skin of fog and thoughts
about the afterlife.
How could anyone be sure,
faith on hold after another one
of God's swipes across our lives,
not a year between.   6/02

Maybe God wasn't in the picture,
maybe he just wanted to be with his father
at any cost,
found a short cut,
no long drawn out affair as his father's death.

But where did he go? we ask,
and then we see it — the snakeskin —
lying softly, drawn out on a weedy bank,
the transparent head still deep
in a hole.

I lift the skin gently, but not
gently enough. It breaks off near the hole.
My daughter starts digging for the head,

69

wants to bring it up
from underground, wants the whole of it.
She reaches in, brings up only the last
of skin thinned to a point.

In the fog we stand on the bank
holding the pieces, having him and not
at once, he already sunning himself
high up.

Flashback

He told me to go for my walk on the beach
he would wait on the bench watching the waves
if not there in the car his back was sore
so hard leaving him for any time the day wore
a cold wind no birds hard corners inside
a rattling couldn't listen to the hardness
ran back to the bench not there
not in the car not in the restroom back
to the bench the car down the beach
perhaps he had fainted the dark sea
swallowed everything even the sky
had he decided to end it all early
the day was growing late
a friend at the seaside café
having a good time asked if she could help
no well yes if she saw him say
stay right there a tan baseball cap
a tan jacket oh to rest to sip a glass of wine
instead of the whole sea
is this how it will be when he is gone
looking for him between gulps of air
I ran the track again bench car water
and then spotted a tan rock wearing the hat
amidst a jumble of others tossed to hold
back the sea he asleep leaning against
oh there you are I cried *you are*
and nestled beside him in the crevice
discovered you can rock someone
even when there is no space
I don't remember it was hard.

9/02

When I was young I fell in love with hands
of maple leaves, rust and mustard
reaching out to catch the summer's death,
their fingertips crisp on skin that longed for any touch.

I loved the sounds of leaves as they skimmed
across the walk, small poems
having their say before the snow.

Today I sit beneath the Chinese elm,
its slivers of leaves ticking my arm before
landing on the patio with a click, longing

11/02

not for any touch, only his, the one
whose fingers rested on the top of my hand
between this life and that.

Gender balanced. That was the big thing.
I had to bring a man, but wasn't the point
there wasn't one? An unattached man, no less.
I looked up, imagining him floating like a blimp
without wires. Would have to figure how
to get him down. "Never mind," my friend said.
"I'll bring an extra," like you would a spare key,
or stray sock. They trickled in under the shady grove,
women with casseroles to titillate the men —
men carrying mineral water, large loaves
of French bread sticking out of paper sacks
to tease the women — all the while
eyeing each other, like picking over fruit.   11/02
I should have left then. After eating,
the leader placed them in circles like little kids,
boys inside, girls outside, you know how it goes.
They had to answer questions to each other
to see if anything clicked between them.
Stupid questions like "Why didn't the man who
commissioned the Mona Lisa like the final product?"
I felt myself smile oddly, turn to the man
before me and answer that he must have been a fool.
Aren't we all, I thought, shifting
to the next position, and when the circle wobbled,
genders unbalanced as they were,
I slipped off between the trees which seemed
content to stand alone, though branches leaned.

Where once they led cattle up canyon to fatten,
steelhead still run to spawn. We straddle
the sides of the culvert toward the brightness of beach
beyond, a light at the end of a long year
with its square little days that held my grief at bay.

Waves climb up and up out of themselves, some twelve,
fifteen feet, higher, one after the other, full of
themselves,
swollen. Pelicans skim the blizzard of foam,
dive unafraid while we back off.

12/02   How do the steelhead make it past those breakers
to the calm of the Arroyo Hondo?
How is it this species does not die like salmon,
but gives birth to trout whose faces and bodies
change in time, then swim back down the deep canyon

past the meadow with its alders
and wide palmed sycamores,
the fragrant bay laurel, past the old barn
with its rusty carriage, past the orchard
to come to this place and leap
transformed like angels into all that water.

And of course he's here, my life's love. He sings
his unfettered abandon, gliding with the pelicans
along the effervescence of wave
just before it breaks.

we did
knew each other just six weeks
before the *I do* part
the health and sickness part
and it came so fast —
three decades together fast —
always said we'd split
when it didn't work
I always the one to leave
get in my car and just away
return with a *sorry*
he never did until he did
sorry to do this his last words   2/03
how I wailed
me now a one
him off doing his soul thing
God knows if he's wind or star
or that damn raccoon come sniffing
around every night
knocking over the garbage
so I have to look at it all
contain it again
I miss his middle
my arms wrapped around
behind him on the Harley
pressed against him not to fly off
me reflected in his helmet
the sun behind
speed kept us together

when I'd dawdle
hiking in the mountains
he'd panic
told me when the sun drops that high up
it's gone just you and the bears
and the mountain lions
he was right just me and them
and now that damn raccoon

Thick in the march, chanting *Peace Yes,*
War No, I reached for my eyeglasses to read
the poster with small letters a distance away
and thought of him, our first encounter late 60's,
outside UCLA's Royce Hall, where he criticized
my play, *What If They Gave a War*
and No One Came. I said I didn't know
what he was talking about, I was leaving and besides
had a terrible headache, because of stress or
Kennedy being shot and Martin Luther King
and he said I probably needed glasses
and made a date to drive me to his optometrist.
I thought of how glasses didn't help   3/03
and criticized his glasses, thick black rims
that made him look like an accountant,
which he was. Next thing, I went blind
in that eye, probably bad karma.
The doctor said I needed rest
so this near stranger, wearing new wire-rimmed
glasses, I noticed, drove me to his place,
to meet his motherless boys who asked me to stay
and make dinner and help with their homework.
In the midst of commotion about war
and peace, we lost our heads,
my vision returned, and I stayed with him
for over thirty years. He needed new glasses,
he told me in the hospital, but no optometrist
would come, and so I read to him,
this man who always saw clearly what was needed,

how together we rode up Sunset Blvd.
in his yellow mustang, with peace flowers
I splotched all over it and he got a ticket
for speeding and complained about my crazy ways
and every cliché took on new meaning,
even the one about love being blind.
Marching forward, I dug my glasses
out of my pocket and read the sign ahead
painted with rainbows, *Make Love Not War,*
and they did until everything blurred,
like now, history repeating itself.

The Widow Thinks about Boxes

For too long I've written about the tearing,
the wear of death, the glare of summer light
in an empty house, the sift through taped cartons
of what to save, as if the right choices
will bring my husband back,
for instance the shoebox of old letters
he sent his parents when he was off
in boarding school. His mother
must have read and re-read them
until her eyes burned before she tied them up
with a string, those letters like
layers of baklava
I placed whole in the recycle bin   8/03
as if they were made of glass
but later retrieved should courage find me one day,
and I might open them to read
he passed his math test, how much he misses them and
longs for the music of blizzards playing against the house.
With a kiss I patted them down
in a memory trunk with dried roses, and latched the lid.

*

Unsure what to do with the concertina
I gave him the Christmas before he died,
the gift he longed for
but could only play once,
a friend tells me to fetch it.

I lift it off the shelf as if it is made of glass,
unsure of this boldness,
what is sacred always held at arm's length.
He shows me how to pull the bellows out for one note,
push in for the next, like breathing
through the hero's pose,
joining earth to sky. And I do it,
make a holy ruckus with this last gift
full of sky with all its weather
and remember a gypsy ancestor played such a box
dancing his way across space.

Who can say where this will go?

Those women that Chagall painted,
the purple ones floating in a sky concocted
of persimmon and fig-colored squares
over crimson catawampus roofs,

roosters posed in off-kilter windows,
I'm like that, detached. To stay grounded
you have to unfasten yourself
from the once true, look around and see what else:

odd emus poke heads through thistledown fog
silver as the brim of my brain as I drive home
at dawn, my husband somewhere out there,   10/03

not in a Chagall black business suit,
maybe just his cowboy hat
where sky bucks its hind legs.
I want some wild color to ride this out,

imagine Chagall's wings on our backs,
and suddenly we're floating, the whole family,
those living and dead, in a parallel sky
above dense green patches of artichoke fields
and grape vines. Once in awhile

we pass each other and wink.
You should hear that rooster crow.

THE WIDOW DOESN'T TAKE ADVANTAGE

He thinks I'm fragile, you know how sorrow
diminishes a woman, turns you to putty,
all that clay and tears.

He doesn't know I've been lifting weights
for awhile. Sometimes the sky. Once
I pulled my child from under a boulder,
cracked that rock in half. But when
he asks if I need some help, some holes
that need patching

I think, maybe just this one time.
There's the spread of pine needles
on the roof, the loose back gate,

gophers to trap making a mess of the garden,
a screen at the base of the house to repair
where skunks come and go at night.

List in hand, he doesn't look up, straightens
his baseball cap, clears his throat and asks
after that? I tell him, *nothing*.

You know the rest.

11/03

Suddenly they're coming out of everywhere,
these coyote widowers, gaunt and lonely,
full of tricks to tease me to their side.
All they want is a friend who grasps absence,
they say, someone to chat with over grilled fish
and fettucini, and by the way
would she mind going dutch.

At first taken aback, I decide it's safer.
Lay down my money at the movies, too,
free to pull my hand from theirs in the dark.
But when they come with roses, their favorite music
and leftover recipes, I get resistant.
It's too early, I say, looking at the full moon.
I don't eat cake, to another.

Now they're ready for the kill, slick back
their phantom hair and offer thrills
I can't imagine even in my wildest dreams.
I remind them of my limits, a hug
now and then, a tiny kiss. Not that I don't long
to curl around another, not that I don't remember

sweet abandon. *You need therapy*,
the disgruntled snap with their scratch and strut.
I prickle, open the door to the wide world
with a *good luck*, though other words lurk
on the brim of my lips. They yip down the path
to their cars, leaving me alone
to be a better half.

1/04

With rain and November freeze, skunks have come
to the comfort of my home, torn the screen
from the crawl space and burrowed in for the long haul.

At first I think it is a prowler trying to break in,
or my husband — after all, I have just dreamed
he returned from the other world, as often wished.

I bolt from bed flashlight in hand,
fear exchanged for curiosity,
the stench of disgust for possibility of miracle.

11/03   In the dream I am not elated but unprepared,
in a dither to be exact, not expecting such a visit
in the middle of the night of my ongoing life,

not much saved but his wallet, all the credit cards
canceled. His old leather motorcycle jacket hangs
in the closet, though, some chicken in the fridge.

Fully awake, I realize there is only the cat
with her disdainful gaze, the smell I will have to ignore
till morning, and the reminder of what is done, is done.

Next day Pest Control tells me for $400 they install
a one way gate for the skunks to exit, entrance impossible.
That and daily checking of activity will solve the problem.

If only it were that simple, no amount of money
capable of locking out grief. I behold the gifts
of fall, all that gold and retreat of green, waft some sage

through the house to disguise the unwanted
and bless the spirits of those who used to live here
as they wander, checking on things the only way they can.

Feeding the Remains

Night has left the garden moist, a perfect time
to feed the roses, first blooms dried,
some clipped to grace the mantle where my dead
keep their smiles no matter what the news.

Morning comes to the rescue.
I collect spade and shovel,
the box of *Rose Bloom* that promises sturdy growth
and begin to release weeds, wild clover, dead leaves
from the drip line. In the churning of soil

a worm wiggles forth, another, their juicy selves
shining against dark earth,
working all night like dreams
that knead the fragments of our lives.

When young, my father and I would dig them
from the mound in back of the tackle shop
near the lake where we fished. I hated
to thread them onto the hook,
hated the slime on my fingers.
Open your eyes, my father would say.
You'll hurt yourself.

When the bobber disappeared,
I'd pull up an empty line swinging against dawn,
grateful my worms had fed some hungry fish
whose shadow scooted off
ahead of ripples' bloom.

5/04

This morning just before waking, my dead step-son,
young and long-haired, not bald
as when he cut himself off, looks troubled
as do my other children. We are at the airport.
They tell me it is time to go. Push me towards the gate
and turn their backs. Digging,

I wonder at my departure, watch the worms
shocked in the light,
turn them under with my thoughts.

THE WIDOW NEARLY DROWNS ON RETURNING TO HER ROOTS

Between cattails and loon calls, I ran to the end of the pier
and jumped in, held breath at the chilly plunge.

Arm over arm I began swimming, so good to feel
weightless again, and headed out past the lily pads

and mosquitoes, no Pacific waves to run up my nose
and make me choke, just the water that holds you up
when nothing else can.

Suddenly everything was shade, not a ripple. The lake
a mirror. I looked across to the hem of trees,
back to shore. The raft, a speck.

To the right and left only water. The sun growing low.
No boat or bird
I gasped
for air...

If I had a panic attack
like the time
during a movie
set on a submarine
deep under the sea, he wasn't going to come rushing in.

8/04

One of those dreams came to me:
I lifted
his head out of a lake,
placed my mouth on his and breathed,
rhythmically. He opened
his eyes and stared at me like a fish.
I awoke in the middle of a dark tangled bed.

This was not the way I would go,
like in a bad movie. Headlines crossed my mind:
Widow Goes Too Far.
Poet Drowns in Her Own Thoughts.
Often, he said, what a good swimmer I was.

I was, I was… rolled over, floated,
breathed in the life I knew as a child, the absence
of worry, trusting everything

would turn out, that my sins would be forgiven,
that wars would cease and water hold me up,

the holy water that caressed me to shore
through light's last brush.
When I climbed out, there came the plaint of a loon.

Birthday Plan

For his birthday we'd get him onto his beloved boat,
even if it took a crane, I said, we'd lift him
onto the wheel chair, roll him to the lobby, carry him
to the ambulance, drive to the harbor, sirens blaring,
run all the red lights and when we arrived,
the Marina gate would be thrown wide and the crane
would lift him over the side to his place at the fore.

This morning driving down 101, I notice my speed
is 85. Everything's blurry. I never go 85
and he never died before. When I told him my plan
there was this look in his eye, something like fear
mixed with there-you-go-again and something else
I couldn't name that made me kiss him a long time,
and the love went so deep I was surprised to find us
still dressed when the nurse rushed in to silence
the beeping machine that fed him blood.

On his birthday, two days later, the wind kicked up
the best swells of the year, boat leaning in just right,
our son at the wheel, our daughter looking out.
Sometimes I think I pushed him over the edge
with my plan but then I hear him whisper
he just found an easier way to come aboard.

7/04

After a great loss — love comes
from many directions
but often cannot find a way to get in

your eyes closed or
looking somewhere above it all

grasses sing your name
but all you hear is swish, swish
you think means *say nothing*

A heart breaks open in front of you
in the face of such a mirror
you look the other way
in shame

perhaps fear you will disappear
if you get close to the fire again
or miss your song

Silly woman, it's been in you
all along
sing back

there is no ending

1/05

No wonder mountains draw us up,
ascending as they are with fault and fury,
a shaking at the core, one plate pushing
against the other. So every summer we'd come
from months of stumble, our eyes fastened on some peak,
and head off, up
breath deepening with each matched step.
We passed sky's fortress of walls, knelt
to the surprise of columbine, and listened
to wind between thin green needles.
When trees gave way
there was only music of feet on rock.
At any given crest, we'd huddle in triumph looking out
and down, something deep within released
from failings left behind. Boldly,
we'd sign our names in the book at the top.

9/05

When I hold a picture of us with nothing behind but sky
I remember your last breath,
how it exploded with such speed it must have reached
instantly the fist of the mountain
you lived beneath as a boy, this mountain
that almost took your life,
the one you often led us up, the one that drenched us,
blew us over, the one our son mounted
                              to send you forth
and when he did a whirlwind bloomed from the ashes,
circled him with a roar and crescendo, then
disappeared. But we know where you are. We do.

from the paintings of Lysandros Mitsotakis

Oktana means poetry at all times.
— Andreas Embirikos

A red this red I only saw days before
placed in a white bowl like the full moon
bloomed above us

the placenta of my son's first child, his daughter.
It jiggled crimson and shining,
this mass of cells become my granddaughter,

a new planet in our sky   10/05
who screamed this red in her mother's firm arms
and from the red pool the doctor drew up
the sac shaped like a hive where she grew
blue as a slip of sky at dawn
thin as dragonfly wings.

To watch your child cut the cord
of his child, separate her from his wife
is the making of a red this red and wet and immense.

When I held my granddaughter,
I noticed her grandfather's dimple mid-chin,
felt him on the back of my neck and then she opened
her gray eyes and drank me in as someone known.
How could I ever let go
or forget such red.

Something Small

Let me write something small
to fit into this large life
or something large
to fit into my small life

or something bold to help me
find strength
like my husband's last breath
or yesterday's red sunset behind
the black peaks

or was it the black peaks
leaning against that vast red wall?

Self inside self, are you dying
like the sun or more alive than ever
waiting for the light?

UNDATED